A

Literature Unit

for

On My Honor

by Marion Dane Bauer

Written by Gail D. Hanna

The author wishes to thank Chris Bainbridge and Alice Arnold for their valuable help.
Illustrated by Sue Fullam

Teacher Created Materials, Inc.
P.O. Box 1040
Huntington Beach, CA 92647
©*1993 Teacher Created Materials, Inc.*
Made in U.S.A.

ISBN 1-55734-426-4

Table of Contents

Introduction 3

Sample Lesson Plan 4

Before the Book *(Pre-reading Activities)* 5

About the Author 6

Book Summary 7

Vocabulary Lists 8

Vocabulary Activity Ideas 9

Vocabulary in Context 10-13

SECTION 1 *(Chapters 1 through 3)* 14-19
- ◆ Quiz Time!
- ◆ Hands-On Project — *Friendship Bracelet*
- ◆ Cooperative Learning Activity — *Cover Puzzle*
- ◆ Curriculum Connections — *History of Starved Rock*
- ◆ Into Your Life — *Friendship Photo Album*

SECTION 2 *(Chapters 4 through 6)* 20-24
- ◆ Quiz Time!
- ◆ Hands-On Project — *Learning About Surface Currents*
- ◆ Cooperative Learning Activity — *Graph It!*
- ◆ Curriculum Connections — *Geography*
- ◆ Into Your Life — *Reading Response Journals*

SECTION 3 *(Chapters 7 through 9)* 25-29
- ◆ Quiz Time!
- ◆ Hands-On Project — *Peer Editing*
- ◆ Cooperative Learning Activity — *Joel and Tony*
- ◆ Curriculum Connections — *Geography*
- ◆ Into Your Life — *Reading and Writing: Making Connections*

SECTION 4 *(Chapters 10 through 12)* 30-34
- ◆ Quiz Time!
- ◆ Hands-On Project — *More About Currents*
- ◆ Cooperative Learning Activity — *Health and Safety: To The Rescue*
- ◆ Curriculum Connections — *Language Arts: Poetry*
- ◆ Into Your Life — *Making Choices*

After the Book *(Post-reading Activities)*

Word Search 35

Any Questions? 36

Book Report Ideas 37

Culminating Activity 38-41

Unit Test Options 42-44

Bibliography of Related Reading 45

Answer Key 46-48

Introduction

A good book can touch our lives like a good friend. Within its pages are words and characters that can inspire us to achieve our highest ideals. We can turn to it for companionship, recreation, comfort, knowledge, and guidance. It can make us laugh out loud, or cry at its tenderness. It can also give us a cherished story to hold in our hearts forever.

In *Literature Units,* great care has been taken to select books that are sure to become good friends!

Teachers will discover the following features to supplement their own valuable ideas:

- Sample Lesson Plans

- Pre-reading Activities

- Biographical Sketch and Picture of the Author

- Book Summaries

- Vocabulary Lists and Suggested Vocabulary Ideas

- Chapters grouped for study with each section including
    - *quizzes*
    - *hands-on projects*
    - *cooperative learning activities*
    - *cross-curricular connections*
    - *extensions into the reader's life*

- Post-reading Activities

- Book Report Ideas

- Research Ideas

- A Culminating Activity

- Three Options for Unit Tests

- A Bibliography

- An Answer Key

We are confident that this unit will be a valuable addition to your planning, and we hope that as you use our ideas, your students will increase the circle of "friends" they have in books!

Sample Lesson Plan

The following suggested lessons are presented as samples only. Use teacher judgement based upon the needs of your students when teaching a literature unit.

Lesson 1
- Introduce and complete some or all of the pre-reading activities found on page 5.
- Read "About the Author" with your students. (page 6)
- Introduce vocabulary list for Section 1.

Lesson 2
- Complete Vocabulary In Context for Section 1. (page 11)
- Work on Cover Puzzle. (page 16)
- Read Chapters 1 through 3.
- Choose one or more vocabulary activities. (page 9)
- Make Friendship Bracelet. (page 15)
- Read about Starved Rock and answer questions. (pages 17 and 18)
- Begin Friendship Photo Album
- Administer the Section 1 Quiz. (page 14)

Lesson 3
- Introduce vocabulary list for Section 2.
- Complete Vocabulary In Context for Section 2. (page 12)
- Read Chapters 4 through 6.
- Conduct the science experiment about surface currents. (page 21)
- Make a graph to compare swimmers to non-swimmers. (page 22)
- Work on geographical terms. (page 23)
- Begin "Reading Response Journals." (page 24)
- Administer the Section 2 Quiz. (page 20)

Lesson 4
- Introduce vocabulary list for Section 3.
- Complete Vocabulary In Context for Section 3. (page 13)
- Read Chapters 7 through 9.
- Work on Peer Editing. (page 26)
- Discuss relationship. (page 27)
- Work on map skills. (page 28)
- Help students see the connection between what they read and what they write. (page 29)
- Administer the Section 3 Quiz. (page 25)

Lesson 5
- Introduce vocabulary list for Section 4.
- Complete Vocabulary In Context for Section 4. (page 14)
- Read Chapters 10 through 12.
- Conduct more science experiments about currents. (page 31)
- Learn about emergency response. (page 32)
- Model, create, and share diamante. (page 33)
- Write about making choices. (page 34)
- Administer Section 4 Quiz (page 30)

Lesson 6
- Complete word search. (page 35)
- Discuss any questions your students might have about the story. (page 36)
- Consider book report ideas. (page 37)
- Begin work on culminating activity. (pages 38-41)

Lesson 7
- Administer Unit Test(s). (pages 42-44)
- Go over Unit Test(s) with your students.
- Allow discussion time for students' reaction to the book.
- Provide a list of related reading for your students. (page 45)

Before the Book

Good readers bring to the reading situation knowledge about the language and the topic. Therefore, prior to reading *On My Honor* with your students, it is important to do some pre-reading activities with them in order to make certain they will enter the reading situation equipped with sufficient preparation. This will ensure that the subsequent reading experience will be a pleasurable and rewarding one. Suggested activities are listed below.

1. Discuss the meaning of the phrase "On My Honor." Your discussion might include mentioning classroom events and happenings in which you expect the children to be on their honor. For example, when you select a student to deliver a message, you expect he or she will do so in accordance with established classroom rules. Encourage your students to think of similar experiences from their own lives that they can share. Have they ever entrusted a friend or neighbor with the care of a pet?

2. Explain what a Newbery Honor book is.

   Every year, one author is selected to receive an award that is known as the Newbery Medal. It is given to the author who has made the most distinguished contribution to American children's literature. A man by the name of Frederic G. Melcher is the person who is responsible for the creation of this award. He named it Newbery in honor of John Newbery who is famous for being the first person to print and sell books that were written just for children.

   Encourage your students to look for Newbery Honor books. They can frequently be identified by the seals on the covers.

3. Read the author page to learn more about Marion Dane Bauer.

4. Starved Rock is mentioned numerous times. Share with the students its historical significance. (pages 17-18)

5. Students must learn strategies to use when they come across an unfamiliar word. One strategy students can use is to substitute a known word for the unfamiliar one. The Vocabulary in Context sheets were designed to help students develop skill in making such substitutions.

About The Author

Marion Dane Bauer was born on November 20, 1938, in Oglesby, Illinois. She lived all her childhood in this small prairie town surrounded by corn fields and woods, with a quarter mile road leading out to the highway. This road took her to school, to the library, to the pool, to ballet lessons, and to the Episcopal Church. With a hobo-style bag of her precious belongings slung on a stick, she would walk down the road to the highway dreaming of what was beyond her small world. She began to write her dreams in stories when she was a teenager.

After attending LaSalle Peru-Oglesby Junior College and the University of Missouri, Marion graduated from the University of Oklahoma in 1962. During this time she married Ronald Bauer and raised two children, in addition to being a foster parent to several children. Marion taught high school English in Wisconsin and creative writing for adults in Minnesota.

All of Marion's novels are based on places she has lived or visited frequently. She sometimes writes of real events in her life and sometimes she writes her dreams. Marion says she mines nuggets from her past, special only to her, and other people treasure them. For *Foster Child* she was awarded the Golden Kite Honor Book for the Society of Children's Book Writer. Other works by Marion include *Shelter from the Wind* and *Tangled Butterfly*.

"For almost as long as I can remember, I have known in some part of myself, that I wanted to be a writer. At first I thought I would be a poet. Stories seemed so long, not to create, but to write out, and I have never, in all my life, won a battle with a pencil. In my hand, a pencil has always been an awkward tool, almost an enemy to be subdued, though in my struggle with points that break and a hand that quickly aches, I am always the loser. In high school I learned to type. From that time on my direction was clear. I begin with a character, a problem, add on the other characters who fill out that person's life. I rewrite many times. When I am through, the novel never quite meets my own expectations so I begin another."

"I hope to go on beginning for as long as I have life."

Something About the Author, 1980

On My Honor

by Marion Dane Bauer

(Dell, 1986)

Tony and Joel share many adventures as best friends. Tony is the daredevil leader while Joel goes along with Tony's crazy ideas. When Tony decides the two boys should go to Starved Rock to climb the bluffs, Joel thinks it is a dumb idea. However, to show Tony that he isn't scared to climb the bluffs Joel agrees to ask his father, knowing that his father will never allow him to go and he'll save face.

The boys ask permission to bike to Starved Rock without mentioning the bluffs. Much to Joel's surprise, his father gives his permission! Joel is on his honor to only bike to the park and back home. As usual, Tony swaps his battered hand-me-down bike for Joel's ten speed and the boys set off on their adventure. Along the way, Tony stops to cool off in the forbidden river. Tony is soon missing. Joel, not knowing that Tony can't swim, assumes Tony is playing a trick on him. Nevertheless, Joel searches frantically and soon realizes that Tony has drowned.

Joel, scared, pretends they went to the park and returned home as promised, while the parents try to find out exactly what has happened to Tony. Joel has to deal with deceit, guilt, and anger. He feels guilty for not being able to help Tony and angry at his father for allowing him to go on the bike trip.

In the end, Joel learns everyone has to live with his choices, that he will have to live with what happened for the rest of his life, and, no matter what he has done, his father will love him.

Vocabulary Lists

On the page are vocabulary lists corresponding to each sectional group of chapters.

Section 1

tingled	betrayed	sewage	irritation
mere	intention	sandbar	chlorine
battered	sizzled	current	mimicked
fender	exuberance	churned	expand
drooling	bounds	shallow	deserted
bluffs	squinting	toppled	winding
decaying	volume	momentum	elaborately

Section 2

glanced	treaded	crested	authority
realigned	deceptively	peering	erect
spewing	barrage	heaving	possibility
flailing	murky	forlorn	dully
resumed	assistance	occasionally	erratic
indistinct	eddying	rigid	lunges
mewing	clarity	wrung	reverberated
	unglued	convulsed	

Section 3

drummed	blob	squatting	dispel
bunchy	intervals	inserts	tinkering
nonchalance	swayed	gruffly	supplication
snitched	gaze	impatience	musky
expelled	skeptical	crumpling	haphazardly
assembled	pudgy	enormous	peered
hesitated	submitting	circulars	
	burbling	limp	

Section 4

scuffing	ached	mumbled	tentatively
mumbled	swished	blurted	clenched
reassure	fiddling	astonishment	murmur
clammy	silhouetted	misjudged	quivering
nostrils	simultaneous	gooseflesh	honorable
concentrate	slight	jig	casual
muffling	indicated	pummel	racking
	vapor	massive	

Vocabulary Activity Ideas

It is important to provide your students with experiences that will increase their understanding of the vocabulary encountered when reading *On My Honor*. Try some of the following activities with your students.

◆ Select a vocabulary word from the chapter read that day. Try to use that word as many times as you can with your students. Be sure to refer back to its use in the story. This modeling activity will help your students add new words to their listening and speaking vocabularies.

◆ Incorporate some of the vocabulary words into your weekly spelling list. Words can be chosen based on patterns, meaning, relevancy to other content areas, or whatever suits the needs of your class.

◆ Choose just one sentence from the day's chapter to closely examine for meaning. Take, for example, this sentence from Chapter 1: "Joel's spine tingled at the mere thought of trying to scale the sheer river bluffs in the state park." Carefully go over each word and, using the chalkboard or an overhead, try to illustrate the sentence and bring it to life!

◆ Use commercially-prepared computer disks designed to easily make crossword puzzles, word searches, and spelling activities.

◆ Try to meet for a few minutes each day with two or three of your students you know have problems with vocabulary. Discuss key phrases, sentences or paragraphs from the day's chapter. Just a few unknown words may radically alter the chapter's meaning for these students. Try to catch them before they get too far into the story and become confused and frustrated.

◆ Students enjoy playing Vocabulary Basketball as a means of reviewing the spelling and definition of each word. Small groups of students will compete as a team against another small group. A reader from one team will select a vocabulary word which he/she will call out to the other team. The person who is up will spell and define the word. If that person is correct, he/she will be given a chance to throw a bean bag into a wastebasket for 3 points. (Spelling and definition each count as one point, and the throw is worth one point.) If the information given is incorrect, the question will go to the other team.

◆ Play a Vocabulary Bingo game. Have each student make a card with 25 boxes and put the numbers 1-25 randomly in the boxes using blue or black ink. Check to be sure they are not in numerical order. Make a copy of the word list you wish to use, cut apart and place in a container. When ready to play, pick a word and describe it by defining it or illustrating it. Students should write the word in box 1. Continue until 25 words are given. Depending upon the abilities of the students, the teacher can either provide the students with a list of words to choose from or expect the students to know them. After 25 words have been given, the students exchange papers. Call out the correct answers and have them put a red X on the boxes that are correct. Have students count the total number of bingos found on the sheet. A perfect paper has 12. The students with the most bingos win.

Vocabulary in Context

cliffs	tricked	rotting	twisting
empty	dribbling	imitated	fell

Directions: Carefully read each sentence, paying close attention to the boldfaced word. Think about what it means. Choose a word that has a similar meaning from the box to place in the blank in order to make a pair of sentences that have the same meaning.

1. Joel and Tony spent their baby years **drooling** on the same toys.

   Joel and Tony spent their baby years _____ on the same toys.

2. Swimming would be better than getting killed on the park **bluffs.**

   Swimming would be better than getting killed on the park _____ .

3. The road to Starved Rock is narrow, hilly and **winding**.

   The road to Starved Rock is narrow, hilly and _____ .

4. When Joel's father said he could go to Starved Rock, Joel felt **betrayed**.

   When Joel's father said he could go to Starved Rock, Joel felt _____ .

5. Once, Tony tried a square and nearly **toppled** off Joel's bike.

   Once, Tony tried a square and nearly _____ off Joel's bike.

6. "My dad says," Tony **mimicked**, his voice coming out high and girlish.

   "My dad says," Tony _____ , his voice coming out high and girlish.

7. Tony rode in both lanes of the nearly **deserted** highway.

   Tony rode in both lanes of the nearly _____ highway.

8. The river smelled of **decaying** fish.

   The river smelled of _____ fish.

Vocabulary in Context

shook	looked	swirling	sometimes
faded	deceivingly	echoed	clearness

Directions: Carefully read each sentence paying close attention to the boldfaced word. Think about what it means. Choose a word that has a similar meaning from the box to place in the blank in order to make a pair of sentences that have the same meaning.

1. Every few strokes, Tony raised his head and **glanced** toward the sandbar.

   Every few strokes, Tony raised his head and _____ toward the sandbar.

2. The echo of his voice sounded like the **indistinct** mewing of a cat.

   The echo of his voice sounded like the _____ mewing of a cat.

3. The surface of the river looked **deceptively** smooth.

   The surface of the river looked _____ smooth.

4. While lying still, Joel was moved from the **eddying** whirlpool to a slower current.

   While lying still, Joel was moved from the _____ whirlpool to a slower current.

5. With terrible **clarity**, Joel could see the river water he vomited.

   With terrible _____ , Joel could see the river water he vomited.

6. A shiver **convulsed** Joel even though the sun was bright and hot.

   A shiver _____ Joel even though the sun was bright and hot.

7. "When somebody drowns." These words **reverberated** through Joel's skull like a scream.

   "When somebody drowns." These words _____ through Joel's skull like a scream.

8. The girl **occasionally** told her friend to be careful.

   The girl _____ told her friend to be careful.

Vocabulary in Context

unconcern	huge	carelessly	lump
eliminate	reverberated	chubby	taken

Directions: Carefully read each sentence paying close attention to the boldfaced word. Think about what it means. Choose a word that has a similar meaning from the box to place in the blank in order to make a pair of sentences that have the same meaning.

1. Joel's heart **drummed** in his ears.

   Joel's heart _____ in his ears.

2. Joel froze his features into what he hoped was an image of innocence, of **nonchalance**.

   Joel froze his features into what he hoped was an image of innocence, of _____ .

3. When he was little, Joel's mom could tell if he had **snitched** a cookie.

   When he was little, Joel's mom could tell if he had _____ a cookie.

4. Tony's clothes were scattered **haphazardly** along the ground.

   Tony's clothes were scattered _____ along the ground.

5. The shadow had been a small **blob** right next to the light.

   The shadow had been a small _____ right next to the light.

6. Bobby clapped his **pudgy** hands and skittered out of the room.

   Bobby clapped his _____ hands and skittered out of the room.

7. Bobby stared at Joel with his **enormous** green eyes.

   Bobby stared at Joel with his _____ green eyes.

8. Joel shook his head trying to **dispel** the fog that had taken possession of his brain.

   Joel shook his head trying to _____ the fog that had taken possession of his brain.

Vocabulary in Context

cloud	smothering	outlined	under-estimated
damp	goose pimples	honest	hesitatingly

Directions: Carefully read each sentence paying close attention to the boldfaced word. Think about what it means. Choose a word that has a similar meaning from the box to place in the blank in order to make a pair of sentences that have the same meaning.

1. Joel's skin felt **clammy** and he was sure the stink of the river came from him.

   Joel's skin felt _____ and he was sure the stink of the river came from him.

2. The stink of the river rose from Joel like a **vapor**.

   The stink of the river rose from Joel like a _____ .

3. He flopped onto his stomach, **muffling** his response with the pillow.

   He flopped onto his stomach, _____ his response with the pillow.

4. Mr. Bates said, "Joel is an **honorable** boy."

   Mr. Bates said, "Joel is an _____ boy."

5. Mr. Zabrinsky stood **silhouetted** in his doorway.

   Mr. Zabrinsky stood _____ in his doorway.

6. Mr. Bates said, "I'm sorry I **misjudged** the situation."

   Mr. Bates said, "I'm sorry I _____ the situation."

7. Joel's skin rippled into **gooseflesh**.

   Joel's skin rippled into _____ .

8. Joel reached his hand out **tentatively** to touch his father's knee.

   Joel reached his hand out _____ to touch his father's knee.

Quiz Time!

1. Why does Joel sometimes wonder why he and Tony stay friends?

_____

_____

2. What does Joel's dad mean when he says to Joel, "You're on your honor?"

_____

_____

3. How does Joel feel when his father gives him permission to ride his bike to the park?

_____

_____

4. What is better about Tony's old hand-me-down bike than Joel's silver ten-speed?

_____

_____

5. Why aren't people allowed to swim in the Vermillion?

_____

_____

6. Why doesn't Joel leave Tony's bike out in the open where anybody could steal it?

_____

_____

7. Tell what you would have done with Tony's bike.

_____

_____

8. Why doesn't Joel want Tony to leave the river and go to Starved Rock?

_____

_____

9. What does Joel challenge Tony to do?

_____

_____

10. Do you think this is a fair challenge? On the back of this page tell why or why not.

Friendship Bracelet

Tony and Joel have been best friends, with their friendship dating back to their baby days. Discuss with your students the true meaning of friendship, the role it plays in their lives, and its fragile nature. Involve your students in making a friendship bracelet to give to a special friend by engaging in the following activity.

Make clay beads, paint and string on rawhide. Use either the cooked salt-and-flour clay recipe or the recipe for quick and easy modeling dough.

Quick and Easy Modeling Dough

- $^3/_4$ cup flour (any kind except self-rising flour)
- $^1/_2$ cup salt
- 1 $^1/_2$ teaspoons powdered alum
- 1 $^1/_2$ teaspoons vegetable oil
- 1 $^1/_2$ cups boiling water
- food coloring

1. Combine flour, salt, and alum in a mixing bowl.

2. Add vegetable oil and boiling water. Stir vigorously with a spoon until well blended. Dough should not stick to the sides of the bowl and should be cool enough to handle.

3. Add food coloring and knead into dough until color is well blended and the dough is the desired tint.

   Makes about 1 cup. Double the recipe for large projects. For groups, mix several double recipes rather than one large amount. This play dough has a smooth texture and takes approximately 15 minutes to make. It dries to a hard finish overnight. Store it in a jar with a tight lid. It does not need to be refrigerated.

Cooked Clay

- $^3/_4$ cup salt
- $^3/_4$ cup non-self-rising flour
- 2 teaspoons powdered alum
- $^3/_4$ cup water
- 2 tablespoons vegetable oil
- food coloring

1. Mix salt, $^1/_2$ cup flour, and alum in a saucepan.
2. Slowly add water while stirring to break up lumps.
3. Place over low heat and cook, stirring constantly, until mixture is rubbery and difficult to stir. It should not be sticky when touched.
4. Add vegetable oil. Stir until blended.
5. Place on a plate or aluminum foil and set aside until cool.
6. Add up to $^1/_4$ cup flour if clay is sticky.

Makes 1 $^1/_2$ cups.

Model like clay. When making beads be sure to pierce holes in the beads before the clay hardens. It hardens in 1 or 2 days. Store in airtight container.

Cover Puzzle

This particular activity serves as a good introduction to cooperative learning for those students whose experience in cooperative learning is limited. Additionally, it can be used to spark a discussion about what *On My Honor* might be about.

In this activity the picture below is used to create a puzzle. You use your own judgement as to whether you want the students to have access to the picture while they are working on the puzzle. The class is divided into small groups of three or four and each group is assigned the task of assembling the puzzle. The group to finish first is the winner. You may wish to color in the picture, mount on tag board and laminate. Make several so you have one for each group of students. Cut the picture into pieces and place in envelopes or baggies or, leave the picture uncolored. Cut into puzzle pieces and place in envelopes or baggies. When the students have it assembled, they can paste it on tagboard or cardboard and color it as a group. Later the groups can share their completed pictures or put them on display.

History of Starved Rock

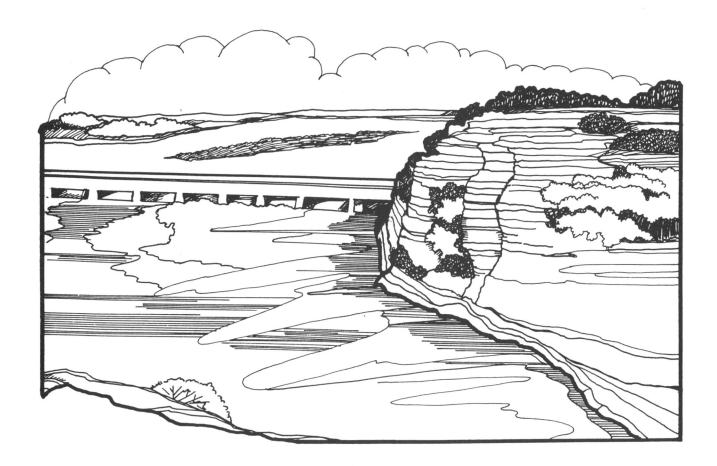

In the year 1911, Starved Rock, located about 90 miles southwest of Chicago on the Illinois River, became the second state park in Illinois. It is famous for its hiking trails which wind past streams and waterfalls throughout eighteen forested canyons. The major attraction of the park is Starved Rock, a 125-foot-high sandstone butte.

According to legend, the existence of the Illinois Indians tribe ended at Starved Rock. The tribe's story was recorded by an early resident of Illinois, Judge John Dean Caton; he heard it from a Pottawattomie chief named Meachelle, who was a boy when the siege took place.

In 1769 the Illinois Indians were being pursued by the Pottawattomies. They tried to escape capture by hiding out on the half acre of land that covered the summit of Starved Rock. Because the sides of Starved Rock were perpendicular, the Pottawattomies did not try to rush in and attack the Illinois Indians. Instead, they would wait until the Illinois Indians' supplies of food and water ran out. When the Illinois tried to lower containers into the river to get water, the Pottawattomies would cut the ropes hoping the Illinois would die of thirst.

Finally, the time came when the Illinois Indians could no longer stay on the summit; many were starving, others had already starved to death. One dark night they decided to escape. Silently, they climbed down the steep hill only to be met and surrounded by their enemy. They did not have the strength to resist and, one by one, the men, women, and children fell. However, not all were destroyed.

Starved Rock *(cont.)*

From high on the summit, eleven of the strongest and most courageous warriors saw where the Pottawattomies had secured their canoes. Suddenly, the eleven brave warriors dashed to the spot, leapt into the enemy's canoes and paddled day and night. The braves did not even take time to stop to search for food, because they knew the Pottawattomies would be after them; to be caught meant sure death.

The escaping Illinois Indians raced for their lives. They believed that if they could make it to St. Louis, they would be safe. When they finally reached the fort, they told their tale to the commandant. He gave them food and promised them protection. Later, when the Pottawattomies arrived and demanded the eleven warriors be turned over to them, their demands were refused. The Pottawattomies left, vowing revenge.

When their enemies were gone, the Illinois very sadly and slowly paddled their way across the river to try to look for new friends among the tribes in the southern part of Illinois. The eleven brave warriors were the only ones left as representatives of what was once a great nation. They are now remembered as part of the past: the "Last of the Illinois."

Here are some post-reading activities you might want to try with your students.

1. Visit a Native American site in your area.

2. Do additional research to find out what happened to the Pottawattomies.

3. Invite a Native American to come speak to the class.

4. Discuss the sadness of what happened and encourage the students to learn about other tales of sadness related to the Native Americans who once lived in their area. For example, the Cherokee who lived east of the Mississippi were forced to give up their homes and ordered to move to Oklahoma. Their 1,000 mile journey became known as the "Trail of Tears" as over 4,000 of the Cherokee died.

5. Have students research some local history in the area in which you live. Share findings with the class.

Friendship Photo Album

Have each student bring in a snapshot that shows him/her with a special friend. The photos will be assembled into an album that has been previously purchased or a simple one consisting of construction paper bound together. Each student will be given a page in the photo album for his/her picture, along with a descriptive paragraph meant to recreate the event(s) portrayed in the picture. The students will also include a cinquain poem about the friend, using the pattern below. Encourage students to be creative when designing the layout of their page. They may wish to design borders for the picture and/ or writing, or they may use the frame provided below. As an extension, students may wish to make their own Friendship Photo Albums, devoting one page to each friend, or the whole album to one special friend.

Cinquain Poetry

Line 1. One word for the title.

Line 2. Two words for a description of the title.

Line 3. Three action words related to the title.

Line 4. Four words to describe the title.

Line 5: One word that is another word for the title.

Friend

Funny, smart,

Laughing, smiling, giving

Sharing and working together

Melanie

Quiz Time!

1. What kind of a swimmer is Tony? Explain your answer.

_____

_____

2. How did Tony once break his arm?

_____

_____

3. When does Joel finally realize that Tony can't swim and has gone under?

_____

_____

4. What makes Joel think that he might die, too?

_____

_____

5. Why doesn't Joel go back into the river to help the boy look for Tony?

_____

_____

6. What do the boy's actions tell us about his character?

_____

_____

7. Why do you think Joel says they are looking for Tony and not a body?

_____

_____

8. How does Joel feel about reporting the drowning incident to the police?

_____

_____

9. Do you think Joel will keep the promise he made to the boy to go to the police?

_____

_____

10. What does Joel imagine Mr. Zabrinsky doing when he discovers what has happened?

_____

Learning About Surface Currents

Tell your students that a current is a flow of moving water or air. Discuss the role of currents in the following excerpts from *On My Honor*.

Every few strokes he raised his head, glanced toward the sandbar, and realigned himself. The current was pushing him downstream and if he wasn't careful he would miss the sandbar entirely.

When Joel dove for the fourth time, letting the current carry him farther from the shore, he found himself caught in the grip of that hurrying water. It sucked at him, grinding him against the silty river bottom.

Have your students work with a partner or in small groups to perform the following science experiment to learn how winds cause surface currents.

Materials: shallow pan, paper hole-punch and one sheet of dark colored construction paper

Procedure:

1. Fill the pan with water.

2. Punch out ten paper circles.

3. Place the circles on the surface of the water near the left side of the pan.

4. Direct your exhaled breath across the surface of the water where the paper is floating.

5. Observe the motion of the paper as you continue to blow.

Results: The paper circles move in a clockwise direction around the outside of the pan.

This happens because your breath starts a surface current (a horizontal movement of water). Surface currents on the earth begin in the tropics when powerful trade winds drive the ocean water before them. The water travels far away from where the wind starts the motion. The surface currents in the Northern Hemisphere move in a clockwise direction, and those in the Southern Hemisphere move counterclockwise. The rotation of the earth, changes in the temperature of the ocean water, and differences in the height of the ocean also contribute to the movement of surface currents.

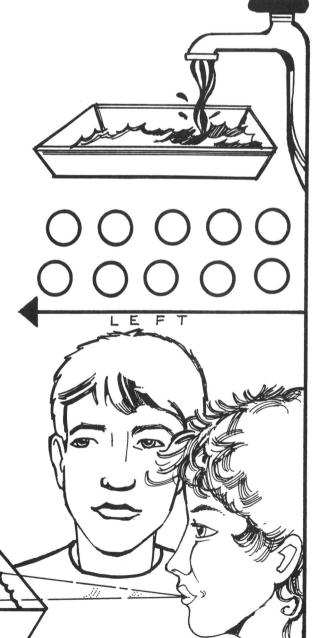

Graph It!

How many students in your school know how to swim? Divide your class into groups and assign each group the task of discovering how many students at each grade level can swim and how many cannot. When all the data is collected, compile for the purpose of using it to make a graph. Each group can create its own graph or create one as a whole class activity. Explore different types of graphing possibilities with your students. Below are some examples of graphs you may want to use.

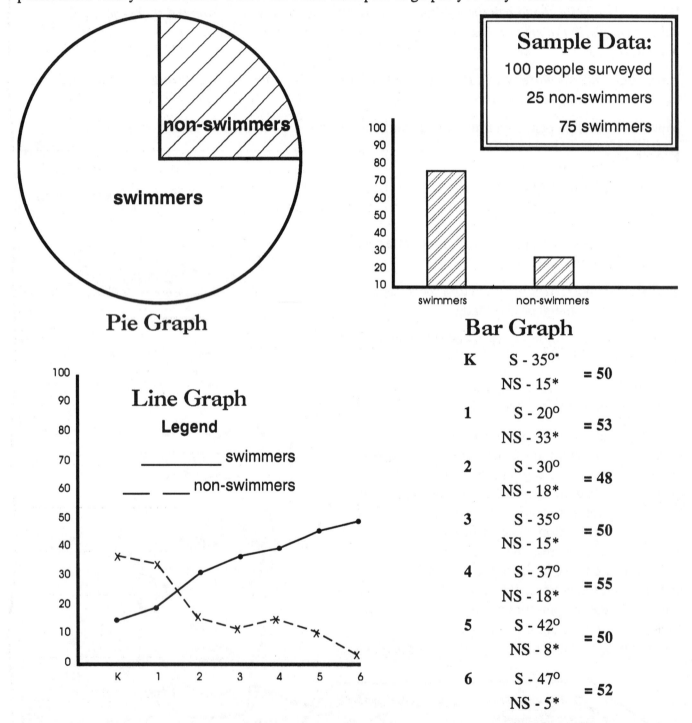

Pie Graph

Sample Data:
100 people surveyed
25 non-swimmers
75 swimmers

Bar Graph

Line Graph

Legend

_____ swimmers

___ ___ non-swimmers

K	S - 35°*	= 50
	NS - 15*	
1	S - 20°	= 53
	NS - 33*	
2	S - 30°	= 48
	NS - 18*	
3	S - 35°	= 50
	NS - 15*	
4	S - 37°	= 55
	NS - 18*	
5	S - 42°	= 50
	NS - 8*	
6	S - 47°	= 52
	NS - 5*	

*It is helpful to assign a symbol designating swimmers vs non-swimmers when collecting data to facilitate the graphing. This type of graph will allow students to observe trends (i.e. as grade level increases the number of non-swimmers decreases)

Geography *(Vocabulary Enrichment)*

Use the following clues to match the geographical terms with their meanings. Write the number of the correct term on the line following each definition.

Old Man River, as a small stream, has its *source* in Minnesota.

The *mouth* of the Mississippi River is in Louisiana where if flows into the Gulf of Mexico.

Tony knew the Vermillion was dangerous because of the strong *currents* which could carry him downstream, the *sink holes* in the bottom of the river, and the *swirling* circles of water. He wanted to stay away from the whirlpools which could suck him under the water.

The author, Marion Bauer, described the Vermillion *River Valley* in the following way. "Joel moved ahead, and when he started down the hill into the Vermillion *River Valley* he leaned forward and pumped, pushing Tony's old bike until it hummed." "Joel reached the bottom of the hill and shot across the bridge so fast that he didn't even get a glimpse of the river below."

Terms

1. source
2. mouth
3. current
4. river valley
5. swirls
6. sink hole
7. whirlpool

Definitions

A. The circular motion of water _____

B. A hole worn through rock by water _____

C. The flow of a river going in one direction _____

D. The beginning of a river _____

E. A swift circular current of water with a lower center which draws in floating objects _____

F. The place where a river flows into another body of water _____

G. The hills and land through which water drains into a river _____

Reading Response Journals

One way to ensure that the reading of *On My Honor* touches each student in a special way is to include the use of Reading Response Journals in your plans. In these journals, students should be encouraged to respond to the story in a number of ways. Here are a few ideas.

1. Tell the students that the purpose of the journal is to record their thoughts, ideas, observations, and questions as they read the book.

2. Provide students with, or ask them to suggest, topics from the story that may stimulate writing. Here are some examples from the chapters in Section 2.

   • The fact that Tony was everybody's friend sometimes made Joel a little bit jealous; he wanted Tony to himself. Describe one instance when you felt jealous.

   • Put yourself in Joel's shoes. Tell about what you would have done when you realized that your best friend had drowned.

   • What reasons do you think Tony might have had for not letting Joel know he couldn't swim? Have you ever pretended you could do something that you really couldn't do?

3. Most students like the idea of having an audience for the material they write, so it is important to provide opportunities for sharing. One way is to have Writers' Circles. In writers' circles students are divided into groups of three or four. The groups meet simultaneously, and the students within each group take turns reading their writing aloud and receiving responses or questions from the others in their circle.

4. Ask the students to draw their responses to certain events or characters in the story.

5. Encourage the students to think of their journal entries as seeds that can be used to generate plays, stories, poems, debates, and art displays.

Allow students time to write in their journals daily. To evaluate the journals, you may wish to use the following guidelines.

Personal reflections will be read by the teacher, but no corrections or letter grades will be assigned. Comments may be made on sticky notes so your students will have your reaction without having their journals permanently marked. Credit is given for effort, and all students who sincerely try will be awarded credit. If a grade is desired for this type of entry, grade according to the number of journal entries completed. For example, if five journal assignments were made and the student conscientiously completes all five, then he or she should receive an "A."

Quiz Time!

1. Write an important question you would ask Joel if you were a police officer and he reported what happened to you.

_____

_____

2. Why does Joel start to ride his bike all the way to Starved Rock State Park?

_____

_____

3. Describe Joel's reaction when he looks at the river and realizes Tony is dead.

_____

_____

4. Why does Joel call his brother, Bobby, a snoop?

_____

_____

5. What lie does Joel tell when his father asked him where Tony is?

_____

_____

6. Why do you think the smell of the river is so strong for Joel, while other people don't even smell it on him?

_____

_____

7. Why were Joel and Tony pooling their allowances?

_____

_____

8. What is Joel going to teach Bobby how to do?

_____

_____

9. How does Joel feel when he sees his parents talking to Mr. and Mrs. Zabrinsky?

_____

_____

10. On the back of this page tell about the plan for getting rich that Joel and Tony had once concocted.

Peer Editing

Read each of the following passages from *On My Honor*. Then select the one you can most vividly imagine. On a separate piece of paper use your markers, crayons, or pencils to make a picture that matches the descriptive passage you chose. When your picture is complete, exchange it with your partner, who will edit it for you.

A. *Joel lay on his back in the middle of his bed staring at the darkened light fixture. The shadow of the fixture stretched across his ceiling like an elasticized gray spider and bent down the wall. When he had first lain down on the bed, the shadow had been a small blob right next to the light.*

B. *Bobby was holding the screen door open for their mother. Looking tired and a little bit frazzled, she set down the grocery bag she was carrying and came to the bottom of the stairs. She stood with her hands on her hips exactly the way Bobby had when he was imitating her earlier. "What on earth were you doing today, Joel? Mrs. Zabrinsky says you and Tony hid in the house all afternoon."*

C. *A squirrel scolded in a nearby tree. The river made a burbling sound, almost as if it were laughing. There were Tony's clothes scattered haphazardly along the ground, exactly where they had been dropped except for the shirt the girl had moved. One sock hung from a nearby bush; the other lay in the midst of a patch of violets.*

A

Is Joel on his back in the middle of his bed?	yes	no
Is Joel staring at a darkened light fixture?	yes	no
Does the shadow of the fixture go across the ceiling and down the wall?	yes	no
Does the shadow look like an elasticized gray spider?	yes	no

Edited by _____

B

Is Bobby holding the screen door open?	yes	no
Is Mrs. Bates standing at the bottom of the stairs with her hands on her hips?	yes	no
Does Mrs. Bates look tired and frazzled?	yes	no
Was a bag of groceries set down?	yes	no

Edited by _____

C

Do you see a squirrel in a nearby tree?	yes	no
Are Tony's clothes scattered haphazardly along the ground?	yes	no
Is one sock hanging from a nearby bush?	yes	no
Is one sock in the middle of a violet patch?	yes	no

Edited by _____

Joel and Tony

Arrange the students in small groups and assign them the task of working together cooperatively to complete the Venn diagram to compare and contrast the two main characters, Joel and Tony. A list of facts and character traits is provided for the students to choose from and they should feel free to add ideas of their own. The purpose of this is to provide the students with a model so they can then pair up with a partner and construct, on separate paper, their own personal Venn diagram. The Venn diagrams created by the students can then become part of a bulletin board display or put together as a class book. This provides all students an opportunity to learn more about each of their classmates.

enjoyed swimming	lied to parents	liked school
small family	liked working on projects	large family
12 years old	careless	delivered papers
neat	cautious	felt guilty
had crazy ideas	drove teachers nuts	enjoyed bike riding
afraid of water	daredevil	building a tree house

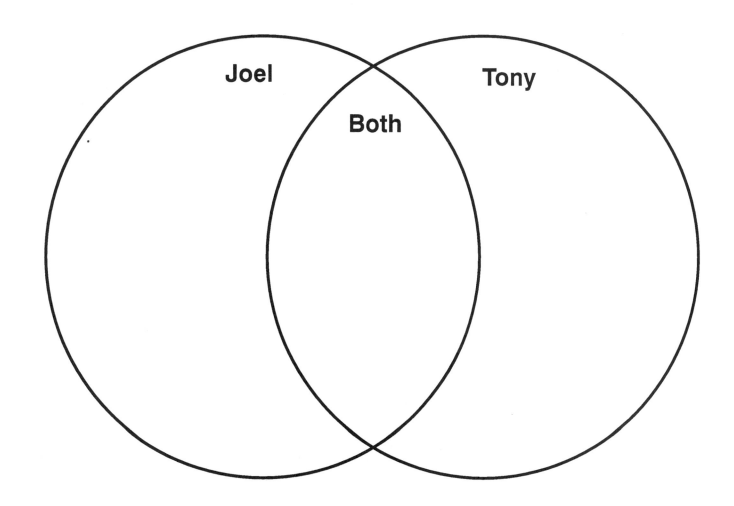

Geography *(Map Skills)*

1. Tony called the Vermillion River "Old Man River." Joel knew this was incorrect. Using the map of the United States, draw in Old Man River and label it with its proper name.

2. Use abbreviations to label the following states: Minnesota, Wisconsin, Illinois, Missouri, Kentucky, Tennessee, Arkansas, Mississippi, and Louisiana.

3. The mouth of Old Man River is in Louisiana where it empties into the Gulf of Mexico. Label the Gulf of Mexico.

4. The source of Old Man River is in Minnesota. Place an X at the beginning of the river. Draw an arrow to show the direction in which the water is flowing.

5. Place a star in the west central part of Illinois where Starved Rock is located.

6. Color the state where you live. A river in your state is _____ .

Reading and Writing: Making Connections

1. Joel's mother once told him he was the worst keeper of guilty secrets in the world. What does this tell us about Joel? What was Joel planning to keep secret? What kind of secret keeper are you? What kind of secret is helpful to keep? What kind might be harmful?

   _____

   _____

   _____

   _____

2. Joel called his brother, Bobby, a snoop because he had told Mrs. Zabrinsky that Joel was hiding in the house. Write a brief paragraph describing an experience either you or an acquaintance had in which you got caught in a lie or in a situation when you were doing something you were not supposed to do.

   _____

   _____

   _____

   _____

3. Joel screamed that he was sick of his stinking paper route and he pushed the remaining stack of papers off the porch. We can tell from Joel's actions that he was angry, and that he took his anger out on the newspapers. Earlier, Joel took his anger out on his little brother, Bobby, when he thumped him on his head with the handle of a knife. Write about a time when you were angry and you took your anger out on someone or something.

   _____

   _____

   _____

   _____

4. Anger is an emotion everyone feels from time to time. The important thing is to learn how to control and express the anger. People who cannot control their angry feelings frequently end up having problems with school, with the law, and with other people. Think of three things a person who is angry could do to help make the feeling go away.

   _____

   _____

   _____

   _____

Quiz Time!

1. What does Mrs. Zabrinsky tell Joel that Tony was afraid to do?

_____

2. Is it easier to remember something you told that was true or something that was a lie? Why?

_____

3. Why doesn't Joel get back into the shower when he doesn't smell clean?

_____

4. How does Joel hold his tongue while his mother talks to him?

_____

5. What reason does Joel have for not telling his mother the truth about what had happened?

_____

_____

6. Tell what the police officers found.

_____

_____

7. Joel said to his father, "I hate you!" Does he really mean it? Explain.

_____

8. What is Joel's father sorry about?

_____

9. Tell what Joel can't make disappear.

_____

10. Describe how Joel feels at the end of the story.

_____

_____

More About Currents

Whirler

The following experiment will demonstrate the effect of the earth's rotation on wind and water currents.

Materials: construction paper; scissors; pencil; ruler; eyedropper

Directions

- Cut an 8 inch (20 cm) diameter circle from the construction paper.
- Push the point of the pencil through the center of the circle.
- Place a drop of water on top of the paper near the pencil.
- Hold the pencil between the palms of your hands and twirl the pencil in a counterclockwise direction.

Observe what happened and discuss possible reasons.

Currents

The following experiment will help students determine if temperature effects the motion of water.

Materials: blue food coloring; 2 clear drinking glasses; 2 coffee cups; jar, 1 quart (liter); eyedropper; ice

Directions:

- Fill half the jar with ice; then add water to fill the jar. Allow to stand for 5 minutes.
- Fill one of the cups one-quarter full with the cold water from the jar.
- Add enough food coloring to the cold water to produce a dark blue liquid.
- Fill one of the glasses with hot water from the faucet.
- Fill the eyedropper with the cold colored water.
- Insert the tip of the eyedropper into the hot water in the glass and release several drops of colored water.
- Observe the movement of the colored water.
- Fill the second glass with cold water from the jar.
- Fill the remaining cup one-quarter full with hot water from the faucet and add enough food coloring to produce a dark blue liquid.
- Fill the eyedropper with the hot colored water.
- Insert the tip of the eyedropper in the cold water in the glass. Release several drops of the hot colored water.

Observe the movement of the colored water. Discuss what happened and possible reasons.

To The Rescue

How much do your students know about water safety? Initiate a group discussion by asking the following questions. Record students responses on chart paper, the chalkboard, or use an overhead projector. After these are tabulated, discuss with your students the proper response to each situation. This exercise presents an excellent opportunity to make arrangements for personnel from the local fire department to talk to the class about emergency care for water-related accidents. Most departments have videos available showing real life episodes of drowning victims who have been resuscitated despite having gone thirty minutes or more without breathing. Additionally, fire department personnel can demonstrate resuscitation techniques using a mannequin and, possibly, set up stations so the students can get some firsthand practice.

1. When Joel realized that Tony had gone under, he dove four different times in an attempt to find him. Was this a good idea?

2. The teenage boy told Joel it took five minutes, and maybe even less, for someone to drown. Do you think even if he had found Tony, it would have been too late?

3. Joel's dad told him that, even if he had found Tony, he might not have been able to save him. Tony was bigger, heavier, and didn't know what he was doing, so he might have pulled Joel under. Do you agree?

4. If Joel had found Tony unconscious and not breathing and managed to bring him to shore, what should he have done next?

5. This would be a good time to check on your students' knowledge of how to respond to an emergency situation that might occur while they are at home. Have your students think of a possible emergency situation that might arise, and have them respond to the following in a pretend call to an emergency dispatcher.

- Location

  Street address _____

  City or town _____

  Directions (cross streets, landmarks, etc.) _____

  _____

- Phone number from which call is being made _____

- Caller's name _____

- What happened _____

  _____

- How many injured _____

- Condition of victim(s) _____

  _____

- Help being given _____

Poetry

Writing poetry provides students with a creative outlet for writing about feelings and their relationships with other people and things. Remind your students of the connection between reading and writing. Reinforce that good reading fosters good writing, and good writing fosters good reading! Introduce your students to a type of poetry called a diamante by implementing the following procedures.

1. Using the chalkboard, overhead, individual copies, etc., share with your students the following example of a diamante.

Truth

Honest, real

Giving, believing, trusting

Church, court, jail, prison

Stealing, taking, cheating

Dishonest, dishonorable

Lie

2. Allow your students ample time to read and reread the poem. Elicit from them remarks about its construction and the relationship between the name for this type of poem and its shape. The students should note the following:

   ✧ The poem is shaped like a diamond; hence the name diamante (dee-ah-mahn-tay).

   ✧ The first and last lines are antonyms.

   ✧ The second line consists of two adjectives describing the subject noun.

   ✧ The third line has all participles describing the subject noun (ing, ed).

   ✧ The fourth line contains four nouns relating in equal measure to both antonyms.

   ✧ The fifth line has all participles describing the antonym of the subject noun.

   ✧ The sixth line consists of two adjectives describing the antonym of the subject noun.

   ✧ The seventh line is the opposite of the first.

   ✧ The words in this poem do not have to rhyme.

3. Do several examples of this type of poem with your students making certain to model for them the thinking process that is involved.

4. Assign the students the task of creating one or more diamantes using a word or an idea that relates to *On My Honor*. You may want to publish a class book displaying the finished products!

Making Choices

Everyday, your students find themselves in situations that require them to make choices. Relating to the poem "The Road Not Taken" by Robert Frost, see page 39, discuss with your students the effect that Joel's and Tony's choices had on their lives. Then have your students read and respond to each of the following situations.

1. What might have happened if Joel and Tony had ridden their bikes directly to Starved Rock?

    _____

    _____

    _____

    _____

2. Joel agreed to go with Tony to Starved Rock because he didn't want Tony to think he was a chicken. What do you think would have happened if he admitted to his fear and refused to go along with Tony's idea?

    _____

    _____

    _____

    _____

3. Suppose you and your best friend are at a birthday party. There are no adults at home and some of the older kids have alcohol. Your friend puts pressure on you to drink because everyone else is doing it. What would you do?

    _____

    _____

    _____

    _____

Word Search

Find and circle the words below in the word search. Then choose five of the words and use them in a paragraph that relates to *On My Honor*.

```
h  o  n  o  r  h  o  e  s  i  m  o  r  p
t  m  p  n  h  o  w  e  c  i  l  o  p  y
t  n  e  r  r  u  c  a  d  o  i  n  e  n
s  w  i  m  m  i  n  g  g  t  k  i  r  e
s  o  d  s  a  y  h  o  w  c  i  p  m  k
u  s  s  a  h  a  e  n  o  a  i  p  i  c
o  t  h  n  i  n  k  r  i  h  e  i  s  i
r  a  r  d  w  e  d  d  i  n  s  s  s  h
e  g  b  b  e  e  l  l  s  v  b  s  i  c
g  e  r  a  v  e  r  m  i  l  l  i  o  n
n  y  s  r  o  o  n  d  u  o  n  s  n  t
a  y  a  o  u  t  h  f  i  n  k  s  w  e
d  t  r  u  s  t  f  l  l  g  o  i  d  b
s  p  u  n  i  s  h  m  e  n  t  m  r  e
```

Starved Rock	honor	trust
sandbar	current	Vermillion
police	punishment	permission
dangerous	Mississippi	bluffs
swimming	chicken	promise

Any Questions?

When you finished reading *On My Honor,* did you have some questions that were left unanswered? Write your questions here.

_____

_____

_____

Work alone, with a partner, or in small groups to prepare possible answers for the questions you asked above and those written below. When you finish, share your ideas with the class.

1. How will Bobby react toward Joel?

2. Will Mrs. Zabrinsky continue to babysit Bobby while Mrs. Bates goes to work?

3. Will Joel talk to Tony's brothers? What will he say?

4. What do you think Tony's brothers might say to Joel?

5. How would events have changed if Tony had been saved?

6. What do you think seventh grade will be like for Joel?

7. Do you think Bobby and Joel will develop a closer bond?

8. What might Mr. Zabrinsky say to Joel?

9. In your opinion, who might believe that what happened was all Joel's fault?

10. If Joel were to write a letter to the Zabrinskys, what do you think it would say?

11. Was Tony's death Joel's fault?

12. Will Joel's father ever trust him again?

13. How do you think Tony's other friends will act toward Joel?

14. What can Joel do to help him cope with his grief?

Book Report Ideas

There are a variety of ways to report on a book once you have read it. When you have completed reading *On My Honor*, select a method of reporting on it that is of interest to you. Use an idea of your own or any one of the following suggestions.

Sales Talk

- This is a sales pitch, aimed at one or more individuals or groups, attempting to persuade them to read the novel *On My Honor*. Be sure to include graphics in your presentation.

Into the Future

- This report predicts what might happen if the author wrote a sequel to the novel. It may take the form of a story in narrative or dramatic form, or a visual display.

A Letter to a Character

- In this report, write a letter to any character in the story. Ask him or her any questions you wish. You may even want to offer some advice on a particular problem.

A Letter from a Character

- In this report, you pretend a character wrote to you with a special request or advice about a special problem or occurrence in his or her life.

Feelings

- In this report you discuss the feelings you had during and/or after reading. Did you laugh? Cry? Get angry? Why? Did the ending leave you feeling satisfied or thirsting for more?

From the View of an Artist!

- This report is a visual one that is a collection of designs, drawings, paintings or some artistic portrayal of major story events and/or characters.

Book Review

- This report is a written summary of the book, along with the writer's recommendations that include both positive and negative features.

TV Commercial

- With other students, as many as necessary, create and perform as TV commercial to sell the book. Make your commercial entertaining and to the point.

Performing

- Act out a scene from *On My Honor*. You may need to ask some fellow students to help you out by being other characters. Explain why you chose the scene and why it is important to the story.

Book Jacket

- You are the publisher of the *On My Honor*. Design a book jacket that will attract attention and encourage people to pick up the book and want to read it.

What Does It Mean To Be Honorable?

Initiate a classroom discussion about what it means to be honorable. The discussion could include specific examples cited in the daily news about both local and famous people who have engaged in both honorable and dishonorable activities. Choose one or more of the activities listed below for your students to complete.

* Provide students with a list of names of famous people to research and have them find out one or more things that each person did that could be considered honorable. Your list might include past presidents, Nobel Prize winners, inventors, authors, etc.

* Set up a bulletin board or a classroom display of articles and/or photographs depicting people doing honorable things. An example might be a newspaper article relaying the events leading up to the rescue of a baby from a burning building You might also want to illustrate dishonorable events. An example might be an article about someone who was fired for cheating on the job.

* Start a debate. Divide the class and have the students decide whether Joel was honorable.

* This might be a good opportunity to talk about, and to establish, a classroom code of honor. The students could give input about occurrences such as lying, cheating, stealing, and what the consequences should be. Specific incidents could be defined, along with definite punishments for infractions.

* Have students write about what they think it means to be honorable. Give recognition for the best essays submitted.

* Set up a system whereby students are recognized and rewarded for deeds that could be deemed honorable.

* Students could be encouraged to actively pursue something in the community that would demonstrate an effort to be honorable.

* Actions speak louder than words. Have each student be responsible for doing at least one honorable deed either at home, in the community, or at school during a prescribed period of time. The specific deed will then be shared with the class at a designated time set aside for this purpose.

* Invite community members and/or arrange for guest speakers to share with the class personal experiences related to honorable feats. Undoubtedly, the police officers, fire fighters, and paramedics have a lot to share.

The Road Not Taken

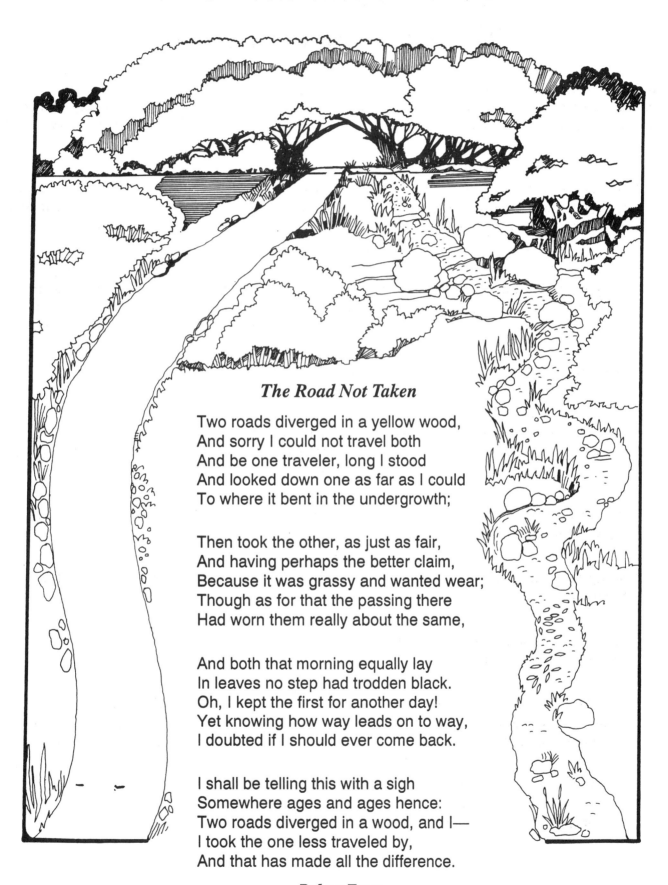

The Road Not Taken

Two roads diverged in a yellow wood,
And sorry I could not travel both
And be one traveler, long I stood
And looked down one as far as I could
To where it bent in the undergrowth;

Then took the other, as just as fair,
And having perhaps the better claim,
Because it was grassy and wanted wear;
Though as for that the passing there
Had worn them really about the same,

And both that morning equally lay
In leaves no step had trodden black.
Oh, I kept the first for another day!
Yet knowing how way leads on to way,
I doubted if I should ever come back.

I shall be telling this with a sigh
Somewhere ages and ages hence:
Two roads diverged in a wood, and I—
I took the one less traveled by,
And that has made all the difference.

Robert Frost

Where The Road Splits....?

After reading "The Road Not Taken," brainstorm a number of events in your life where you were faced with important decisions. Review your list, and select what you feel was a major decision. Next, on a separate sheet of paper, write about how things might have been different if you had made a different choice.

Decisions I Have Made Today:

_____

_____

_____

_____

Decisions I Have Made in the Past Year:

_____

_____

_____

_____

Decisions I Have Made in My Life:

_____

_____

_____

_____

_____

_____

Put a star next to the decisions you feel were major life decisions.

Friendship Tree

Have each student create something that symbolizes friendship to hang on the tree. Listed below are suggested items to hang on the tree. Encourage students to be creative and think of different ideas.

Suggested Projects

- Write a poem or essay entitled "What Friendship Means to Me."
- Write out recipe cards for friendship.
- Make links to a paper chain listing friends' names and why you like them.
- Draw a picture of a friend.
- Make a list of famous friends or partners.
- Make an acrostic using the letters of a friend's name.
- Make friendship bracelets. (See page 15.)
- Wrap a small box containing a list or pictures of gifts you would like to give your friend.
- Write about how you met your friend.
- Make a heart-shaped collage with pictures or words that describe your friend.

How To Make the Friendship Tree

A tree can easily be constructed from two large pieces of corrugated cardboard. Cut both pieces into the shape of a tree with a wide trunk. Take one of the trees and make a center slit halfway down from the top. Take the remaining tree and make a center slit halfway up from the bottom. Then slide the two slit trees into one another. Use thread, yarn, string, wire, or ornament hangers to hang the various objects on the tree.

Unit Test

Multiple Choice: Circle the best answer for each question.

1. What kind of a swimmer was Tony?

  A. excellent   B. good   C. fair   D. poor

2. How did Joel feel when his father gave him permission to ride to Starved Rock?

  A. happy   B. worried   C. sad   D. betrayed

3. Why didn't Joel tell his mother the truth about what had happened?

  A. He was afraid to face the Zabrinskys, the police, and his father.

  B. He was hoping that Tony still might be alive.

  C. He refused to believe what had happened.

  D. He didn't think his mother would believe him.

4. Whom did Joel mostly blame for the events that occurred?

  A. himself   B. his dad   C. Tony   D. Mr. and Mrs. Zabrinsky

5. Why did Joel agree to go swimming in the river?

  A. He thought it would be good practice.

  B. Swimming in the river would be a new experience for him.

  C. He wanted to find out if it really was as dangerous as people claimed.

  D. He didn't want Tony to think he was chicken.

True or False: Write true or false next to each statement.

1. _____ Joel was looking forward to climbing the bluffs.

2. _____ Joel sometimes wished he and Tony were brothers.

3. _____ Tony always told his parents the truth.

4. _____ Mr. Bates trusted Joel.

5. _____ Joel proved he was deserving of his dad's trust.

6. _____ Bobby liked to help his big brother, Joel.

7. _____ Mr. Zabrinsky cried when he found out what happened to Tony.

8. _____ Mrs. Zabrinsky gave Tony permission to ride to the park.

9. _____ Joel and Tony were best friends.

10. _____ The police found Tony's clothes and his bike near the bluffs.

Essay: Use the back of this paper to answer the questions below.

What was Joel's and Tony's relationship like?

How did Tony's death affect Joel's life?

Response

Explain the meaning of each of these passages from *On My Honor.*

Chapter 1:   *"On my honor," Joel repeated, and he crossed his heart, solemnly, then raised his right hand. To himself he added, "The only thing I'll do is get killed in the bluffs, and it'll serve you right."*

Chapter 2:   *"No, you're not. Old Man River is the Mississippi. That's nothing but the Vermillion down there."*

Chapter 3:   *"We'll see who's chicken," Joel said.*

Chapter 4:   *"You sure you'll make it?" Joel eyed his friend's still faintly heaving chest meaningfully. "You look pretty tired to me."*

Chapter 5:   *"We're not looking for a body," Joel said, turning back fiercely. "It's Tony we're looking for!"*

Chapter 6:   *For an instant Joel couldn't breathe. His throat closed, and the air was trapped in his chest in a painful lump. He lifted his hands in surprise, in supplication, but when the breath exploded from him again it brought with it a bleating moan.*

Chapter 7:   *Joel pulled the shirt off, got another from the drawer. The new shirt was fresh—it smelled like his mom's fabric softener—but the light fragrance couldn't cover the stench of the river clinging to his skin.*

Chapter 8:   *Joel stuffed and rolled, the fury taking over again, but this time he knew whom he wanted to punch. It was all Tony's fault. All of it! Tony knew what a poor swimmer he was. He had to have realized the risks. And now he had gone off and left Joel to answer for him. And what was he going to say.*

Chapter 9:   *"I suppose I shouldn't worry," Mrs. Zabrinsky replied, "But you know what Tony's like. I guess I worry more about him than all the rest of the kids rolled up together."*

Chapter 10:   *Honorable? Joel staggered beneath the weight of his father's arm, then pulled away, teetering on the edge of the porch. The five faces bent toward him were like five pale moons, but it was his father's face that loomed the largest.*

Chapter 11:   *"Make it go away," Joel spoke in a whisper, as if they were discussing another person standing in the room, someone who could be forced to leave. His father smoothed the hair back from Joel's face. "I can't," he said, very quietly.*

Conversations

Work in size-appropriate groups to write and perform the conversations that might have occurred in the following situations:

- Joel tells Tony he doesn't want to ride to Starved Rock. *(2 people)*

- Joel's dad tells the boys they should not ride their bikes to Starved Rock. *(3 people)*

- Tony tells Joel he is afraid to swim. *(2 people)*

- A stranger at the river sees the boys going into the water and warns them. *(3 people)*

- The teenagers tell their friends about what happened at the river. *(3 or more people)*

- Tony comes out of the bushes and tells Joel he was only playing a trick; he didn't drown. *(2 people)*

- Joel goes to the police station to report that Tony has drowned. *(2 or more people)*

- Joel goes to Tony's house to tell his parents what happened. *(3 people)*

- Joel's parents and Tony's parents try to figure out where Tony is. *(4 people)*

- Joel apologizes to Bobby for losing his temper. *(2 people)*

- Tony's parents tell his brothers what has happened to Tony. *(4 or more people)*

- Tony's brothers talk to Joel about the incident at the river. *(3 people)*

- School starts in the fall and Joel talks to the coach about joining the swim team. *(2 people)*

- Joel talks to the school counselor about his grief. *(2 people)*

- Joel has a one-sided conversation with Tony after his death. *(1 person)*

Related Reading

The following books have been selected based upon their relationship to the themes dealt with in *On My Honor*. Encourage your students to select a book from this list for pleasure reading. You may want to give them a copy of this list to take with them when they go to the library.

The Death of a Friend

Aaron, Chester. *Spill*. Atheneum, 1977. Ages 12-14.

Brooks, Jerome. *Make Me A Hero*. Dutton, 1980. Ages 9-12.

Cohen, Barbara, Nash. *Thank You, Jackie Robinson*. Lothrop, 1988. Ages 10-13.

Greene, Constance Clarke. *Double-Dare O'Toole*. Puffin, 1990. Ages 9-11.

Paterson, Katherine Womeldorf. *Bridge to Terabithia*. Crowell, 1977. Ages 9-12.

Smith, Doris Buchanan. *A Taste Of Blackberries*. Harper, 1988. Ages 8-11.

White, Elwyn Brooks. *Charlotte's Web*. Harper-Trophy, 1974. Ages 8-12.

Peer Relationships

Bach, Alice Hendricks. *The Meat In The Sandwich*. Harper, 1975. Ages 10-13.

Blume, Judy Sussman. *Deenie*. Dell, 1991. Ages 10-12.

Bulla, Clyde Robert. *Last Look*. Crowell, 1979. Ages 8-10.

Franco, Marjorie. *So Who Hasn't Got Problems*. Houghton, 1979. Ages 10-12.

Greene, Bette. *Get On Out Of Here, Phillip Hall*. Dial, 1981. Ages 9-12.

Hassler, Jon Francis. *Four Miles To Pinecone*. Fawcett, 1989. Ages 10-14.

Perl, Lila. *Me and Fat Glenda*. Clarion, 1979. Ages 9-12.

Peer Pressures

Bates, Betty. *Tough Beans*. Dell, 1992. Ages 10-13.

Cole, Sheila R. *Meaning Well*. Watts, 1974. Ages 9-12.

Giff, Patricia Reilly. *Poopsie Pomerantz, Pick Up Your Feet*. Dell, 1990. Ages 8-11.

Greenburg, Jan. *The Iceberg And Its Shadow*. Farrar, 1989. Ages 10-12.

Friendship: Best Friend

Adelman, Bob and Susan Hall. *On And Off The Street*. Viking Press, 1970. Ages 8-10.

Ames, Mildred. *What Are Friends For?* Little, 1979. Ages 9-11.

Bonsall, Crosby Newell. *The Goodbye Summer*. Morrow, 1979. Ages 9-11.

Capron, Jean F. *Just Good Friends*. Avalon, 1990. Ages 11-13.

Carrick, Carol. *Some Friend!* Houghton, 1979. Ages 9-12.

Foley, June. *It's No Crush, I'm In Love!* Delacorte, 1982. Ages 11-13.

Girion, Barbara. *Like Everybody Else*. Scribner, 1980. Ages 10-13.

Perl, Lila. *Hey, Remember Fat Glenda?* Clarion, 1981. Ages 9-12.

Feelings of Guilt

Blume, Judy Sussman. *Tiger Eyes*. Dell, 1982. Ages 11 and up.

Byars, Betsy Cromer. *Goodbye, Chicken Little*. Harper, 1990. Ages 9-11.

Estes, Eleanor. *The Hundred Dresses*. Harcourt, 1974. Ages 8-10.

Farley, Carol J. *The Garden Is Doing Fine*. Athenuem, 1975. Ages 11 and up.

Gold, Sharlya. *Amelia Quackenbush*. Seabury, 1973. Ages 10-13.

Holms, Nancy. *Nobody's Fault*. Bantam, 1990. Ages 10-12.

Shreve, Susan Richards. *Family Secrets: Five Very Important Stories*. Knopf, 1979. Ages 9-11.

Zindel, Paul. *The Pigman*. Harper, 1968. Ages 12 and up.

Other Books By Marion Dane Bauer

A Dream Of Queens And Castles Houghton, 1990.
Foster Child Seabury, 1977.
Rain Of Fire Clarion, 1983.
Touch The Moon Dell, 1990
Shelter From The Wind Clarion, 1979

Answer Key

Page 10

1. dribbling
2. cliffs
3. twisting
4. tricked
5. fell
6. imitated
7. empty
8. rotting

Page 11

1. looked
2. faded
3. deceivingly
4. swirling
5. clearness
6. shook
7. echoed
8. sometimes

Page 12

1. reverberated
2. unconcern
3. taken
4. carelessly
5. lump
6. chubby
7. huge
8. eliminate

Page 13

1. damp
2. cloud
3. smothering
4. honest
5. outlined
6. underestimated
7. goose pimples
8. hesitatingly

Page 14

1. Tony rarely felt like doing anything Joel wanted to do.
2. Joel's dad trusted him to do what he said he was going to do.
3. Joel felt betrayed and trapped.
4. It was perfect for doing wheelies and going off ramps.
5. The Vermillion is dangerous. It has sink holes, currents and whirlpools.
6. Tony might never get another one.
7. Answers will vary.
8. Joel didn't want to go and he didn't want Tony climbing the bluffs by himself.
9. Joel challenged Tony to swim out to the sandbar.
10. Answers will vary.

Answer Key *(cont.)*

Page 20

1. Tony was a poor swimmer. When Joel looked at him, he noticed that Tony was splashing wildly, puffing and spewing water, and his hands were flailing.

2. Tony once jumped out of his upstairs window with a sheet tied to his waists and ankles. He claimed to be an expert at hang gliding.

3. When Joel stepped off into the nothingness of the deep water and it felt as though the river bottom was not there, he knew that Tony had gone under.

4. His lungs hurt and he couldn't breathe.

5. The memory of what almost happened to him when the current held him down caused him to be too scared to move.

6. Answers will vary.

7. Joel doesn't want to face the reality that Tony is dead.

8. Answers will vary.

9. Answers will vary.

10. He imagines Mr. Zabrinsky coming to get him, maybe with his leather belt.

Page 23

A. swirls (5)

B. sink hole (6)

C. current (3)

D. source (1)

E. whirlpool (7)

F. mouth (2)

G. river valley (4)

Page 25

1. Answers will vary

2. He was afraid to go home.

3. Joel couldn't breathe. Air was trapped in his chest in a painful lump. He lifted his hands up, then clutched himself and swayed.

4. Bobby had told Mrs. Zabrinsky that the boys had spent the afternoon in the house.

5. He said that Tony went to Starved Rock alone.

6. Answers will vary.

7. They were planning on buying a worm farm.

8. Joel was going to teach Bobby how to swim.

9. Joel was scared, worried.

10. They once planned to sell flattened pennies; also accept their plan to buy a worm farm.

Page 27

Joel
enjoyed swimming
liked school
cautious
small family
neat
felt guilty
Tony
large family
afraid of water
careless
daredevil
had crazy ideas
drove teachers nuts
Both
12 years old
delivered papers
liked working on projects
enjoyed bike riding
lied to parents
building a tree house

Answer Key *(cont.)*

Page 30

1. Tony was afraid to swim.
2. It's easier to remember the truth.
3. He knew it wouldn't help any.
4. He held his tongue tightly between his teeth.
5. He didn't want to have to tell the Zabrinskys, the police, and his father.
6. They found Tony's clothes and his bike.
7. No, Joel was expressing his anger over what happened.
8. He was sorry he had given Joel permission to go. He misjudged the situation.
9. Joel couldn't make the smell of the river go away; it was etched in his memory.
10. Answers will vary.

Page 31

What Happens: The water drop swirls around the paper in a clockwise direction.

Why? The free-moving water is thrown forward, and the spinning paper moves out from under the water. Wind and water currents in the Northern Hemisphere are turned toward the right because of the rotation of the earth. Like the spinning paper, the moving earth moves out from under the unattached air and water, causing them to change direction. The deflection in the motion of objects due to the earth's rotation is called the coriolis effect.

What Happens: The hot colored water will rise in the cold water, and the cold colored water will sink in the hot water. Why? Cold water contracts (gets closer together). Hot water expands (moves farther apart). This makes a drop of cold water more dense than a drop of hot water, because the molecules occupy less space. The denser cold water sinks and the less dense hot water rises. Convection currents are the results of water and air movement due to changes in temperature.

Page 32

1. No. Joel could easily have turned into a victim. A person should not attempt a water rescue unless he/she is a very good swimmer and trained in water rescue. Discuss with your students the events in the book which describe Joel's near-drowning.
2. The concept of drowning in five minutes or less is no longer valid. It is now known that patients in cold water can be resuscitated after 30 minutes, or more, in cardiac arrest. If Joel's initial response had been to immediately get help from emergency care personnel, Tony might have been saved.
3. Answers will vary.
4. Mouth-to-mouth resuscitation and CPR if needed.

Page 35

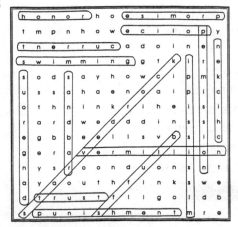

Page 42

1.D	2.D	3.A	4.A	5.D

Essay: Accept appropriate responses

True or False

1.F	2.T	3.F	4.T	5.F
6.T	7.T	8.F	9.T	10.F

Page 43

Accept appropriate responses.